LEGENDS OF WOMEN'S GYMNASTICS

BY EMMA HUDDLESTON

T0015143

Copyright © 2021 by Press Room Editions. All rights reserved. No part of this book may be used or reproduced in any manner whatsoever, including internet usage, without written permission from the copyright owner, except in the case of brief quotations embodied in critical articles and reviews.

Book design by Sarah Taplin
Cover design by Sarah Taplin

Photographs ©: AP Images, cover (left), 1 (left); The Yomiuri Shimbun/AP Images, cover (right), 1 (right); Charlie Riedel/AP Images, 4; Keystone/Hulton Archive/Getty Images, 7; Allsport UK/Getty Images Sport Classic/Getty Images, 9; Heinz Kluetmeier/Sports Illustrated/SetNumber: X20682/Getty Images, 11; Suzanne Vlamis/Stf/AP Images, 12; Elise Amendola/AP Images, 15; John Gaps III/AP Images, 17; Sue Ogrocki/AP Images, 19; Slpa/AP Images, 20; Amy Sancetta/AP Images, 23; Julie Jacobson/AP Images, 24; Kunihiko Miura/Yomiuri Shimbun/AP Images, 27; Dmitry Lovetsky/AP Images, 28

Press Box Books, an imprint of Press Room Editions.

ISBN
978-1-63494-283-6 (library bound)
978-1-63494-301-7 (paperback)
978-1-63494-337-6 (epub)
978-1-63494-319-2 (hosted ebook)

Library of Congress Control Number: 2020913875

Distributed by North Star Editions, Inc.
2297 Waters Drive
Mendota Heights, MN 55120
www.northstareditions.com

Printed in the United States of America
012021

About the Author

Emma Huddleston lives in Minnesota with her husband. She enjoys writing children's books, running, hiking, and swing dancing. After learning about these legends in women's sports, she hopes young people feel empowered to be the best they can be.

TABLE OF CONTENTS

CHAPTER 1

Growing the Sport 5

CHAPTER 2

Raising the Bar 13

CHAPTER 3

New-Era Gymnasts 21

Milestones ▪ 30

Glossary ▪ 31

To Learn More ▪ 32

Index ▪ 32

GROWING THE SPORT

Simone Biles posed in the corner of the floor. Jazzy music filled the arena. It was the 2019 US Championships. And the superstar American gymnast was about to make history.

In an instant, Biles began racing toward the far corner. She performed a roundoff into a back handspring. Then she exploded into the air. The 4'8" gymnast flew 10 feet (3 m) into the air, spinning three times to her side and flipping backward twice. Finally, her feet hit the mat with just a

Simone Biles performs on the uneven bars at the 2019 US Championships.

small hop on the floor. Biles had completed the skill known as a triple-double. No woman had previously done that in competition.

Biles was no stranger to making history. In fact, just two days earlier she had introduced another new skill, the double-double dismount on balance beam. Biles has four skills named for her because she was the first to do them in international competition. Just as impressive is her medal count. Combining extremely difficult gymnastics skills with elite execution, Biles won four Olympic gold medals in 2016. And no gymnast, male or female, has matched her 19 world titles.

Biles's high-flying athleticism stands out today. It would have been totally foreign at the

Larisa Latynina competes on the floor at the 1964 Summer Olympics in Tokyo, Japan.

1928 Olympics, the first to feature women's gymnastics. In fact, even the events were different. It wasn't until the 1952 Games that women first used the four apparatuses that are part of all modern competitions.

Women from the Soviet Union often starred in the early years. Their performances were often graceful and elegant. Larisa Latynina competed in the Olympics in 1956, 1960, and 1964. During her career, she won 18 Olympic medals. That was the record for any sport for nearly 50 years.

Olga Korbut became the sport's first big star

SPEAKING OUT

No woman dominated the 1960s quite like Věra Čáslavská. The Czech star won 11 medals in three Olympics between 1960 and 1968. As of 2020, no woman had won back-to-back all-around titles since she did in 1964 and 1968. However, her career was cut short when she spoke out for political reasons. The Czech government banned her from competing and coaching.

Olga Korbut was the fan favorite of the 1972 Summer Games in Munich, West Germany.

at the 1972 Summer Olympics in Munich, West Germany. Many people viewed Soviet athletes as being cold and robotic. Korbut was different. The 17-year-old cried when she made a mistake in the all-around final. Fans rallied behind her. Then she dazzled fans with her near-perfect gymnastics.

Korbut left Munich with four medals, three of them gold. She became known for her daring skills. She was the first to do a backward somersault on the beam. And the Korbut flip on the uneven bars was one of the most difficult moves in the sport's history. It required the gymnast to stand on top of the high bar. Eventually, it was banned for being too dangerous.

Going into the 1976 Summer Games in Montreal, Canada, no Olympic gymnast had ever scored a perfect 10. Most people believed it was a near-impossible score. In fact, the scoreboards were not even equipped to display anything higher than 9.9. Then Nadia Comăneci arrived.

The Romanian gymnast was only 14 years old. Her performance in Montreal, however,

Nadia Comăneci made history with her performance in Montreal.

showed she was polished beyond her years. One reporter described her not only as an athlete, but also an "artist." And with a flawless uneven bars routine, Comăneci scored a perfect 10. It was one of seven she would score during those Olympics. She went on to win nine medals over two Olympics. The only individual event she never won was vault.

CHAPTER 2

RAISING THE BAR

Gymnasts such as Olga Korbut and Nadia Comăneci helped popularize the sport in the 1970s. In 1984, the Olympics were coming to Los Angeles. American fans were eager to cheer for a hometown gymnastics star. Mary Lou Retton filled that role perfectly.

A native of West Virginia, she moved to Texas to better prepare for the Olympics. She developed a fast, powerful style that differed from the more graceful gymnastics that had been popular at

Mary Lou Retton reacts after sticking the landing on her vault.

the time. By the 1984 Summer Olympics, she was ready.

All eyes were on the all-around competition, in which no US woman had ever won Olympic gold. But after three rotations, Retton was in strong position. Everything came down to vault.

Retton barreled down the runway and pushed off the horse. She took a small step after landing. This cost her points. She had a second chance. But she needed a perfect score to win. She took a breath and ran. She stuck the landing and swung her arms up. Then she pumped her fists in the air, knowing she had nailed it. Retton had won the gold medal!

American gymnastics took off after that. Shannon Miller made her Olympic debut in

Shannon Miller performs her gold medal–winning routine on the balance beam at the 1996 Olympics.

1992, winning five medals. But it was the 1996 Olympics in Atlanta where the US team took it to the next level. Miller was back to lead the group. On home soil in Atlanta, Georgia, she became the first US gymnast to win gold on balance beam. However, teammate Kerri Strug stole the show.

Strug and Miller were part of a team nicknamed the Magnificent Seven. Many believed they could win team gold. The United States had never done that. However, the competition was close. Team USA ended on the vault. Strug was the last to compete.

When she landed her first vault, Strug fell. She felt something snap in her ankle. Pain surged through her body. Yet she soon lined up for her second vault. This time she nailed it, though she could barely put any weight on

Kerri Strug grimaces as she lands on her injured ankle during the 1996 Olympics.

her injured leg. Fans were taken by Strug's poise. Her performance helped seal the team gold medal.

AMÂNAR VAULT

Today's gymnastics fans might be familiar with the Amânar vault. With a roundoff onto the horse and then a backflip with 2.5 twists, it's one of the most difficult skills in the sport. Gymnasts such as McKayla Maroney and Simone Biles mastered it in the 2010s. But the skill was invented two decades earlier by Romanian Simona Amânar. She won seven medals over two Olympics. They included vault gold in 1996 and team and all-around golds in 2000.

Svetlana Khorkina was on the Russian team that took silver in 1996. Early in her career, she was known as "Queen of the Bars." She won the Olympic gold medal in that event in 1996 and 2000. But Khorkina also developed into a top all-around gymnast. She introduced new skills on each apparatus. She also became the first to win three all-around world titles, though she never won the all-around at the Olympics.

Svetlana Khorkina dominated the bars, then became a well-rounded competitor.

Beïjing 2008 ᗄᗄᗄ

CHAPTER 3

NEW-ERA GYMNASTS

Gymnastics entered a new era in 2006 with the debut of a new scoring system. Two American stars were among the first to compete under the new system.

Shawn Johnson, a short and powerful gymnast from Iowa, won the all-around world title in 2007. But Nastia Liukin had been world class for years, too. The daughter of Russian gymnasts, Liukin grew up in Texas and became known for her more classic style. Her long, graceful

Shawn Johnson displays her championship form on the beam at the 2008 Olympics.

lines showed off her technique. Most expected one of the two would win the all-around title at the 2008 Olympics. The question was which one?

Through three rotations, the scores were close. Johnson posted a better score on vault. But Liukin took the lead after strong bars and beam routines. Johnson was in third. It all came down to the floor exercise.

Liukin went first, and her routine was nearly perfect. But Johnson was the defending world champion on floor. She roused fans with her energy and tumbling. In the end, both posted the same score on floor. Liukin won gold in the all-around by just 0.6 points. Johnson took silver and later won gold on the balance beam.

Nastia Liukin held on to win the all-around gold in 2008.

That wasn't the only fierce rivalry in 2008. China was competing on home soil in Beijing. Gymnastics had long been popular there, but China had never won the team title. Led by the popular Cheng Fei, they finally did, holding off a strong US team. Cheng had won three vault world titles and one on floor in the years prior. In Beijing, she also won bronze medals on vault and beam.

Liukin's all-around gold medal was the second in a row for an American. In 2010, few were expecting Gabby Douglas to be the one to extend that streak. But she was determined. That year she moved from her home in Virginia to train with Johnson's coach in Iowa. Douglas was just 14. She missed her family and even

Gabby Douglas came out of nowhere to win gold in the all-around in 2012.

CHUSO KEEPS ON CHUGGING

Since the 1970s, the top gymnasts at the Olympics and World Championships have tended to be teenagers. Younger bodies are often more flexible and lightweight. This makes some moves easier. Also, the wear and tear of intense training takes a toll over time.

Despite all that, Oksana Chusovitina, who is often called "Chuso," qualified for the 2021 Olympics. It marked her eighth Olympics Games. She was already the oldest female gymnast in Olympic history. Chuso has represented the Soviet Union, Germany, and Uzbekistan. She's won a gold and silver medal.

thought about quitting. But her mom encouraged her to stick with it, and the move paid off.

By the Olympic year in 2012, Douglas was ready to shine. She finished second in the all-around at the US Championships. Then she won at the Olympic trials. Her high-flying uneven bars routine always scored high. Douglas was also strong in the other events. And at the Olympics, everything came together for her. Douglas became the first Black gymnast to win Olympic

Vault specialist Oksana Chusovitina was still going strong at age 44.

all-around gold. She also extended the US winning streak in the event to three straight. The streak began with Carly Patterson in 2004.

Aly Raisman might have been the one to push that streak to four in 2016 if not for otherworldly teammate Simone Biles. Raisman had been the captain of the 2012 team, which

Aly Raisman, *left*, and Simone Biles were each other's biggest supporters at the 2016 Olympics.

won the gold medal. She also won the floor exercise gold, took bronze on beam, and was fourth in the all-around.

Four years later, both Raisman and Douglas made the US team. They again won team gold medals. The question was who would join Biles in the all-around final. Both were good enough, but only two per country could qualify. Douglas had the third-best qualifying score overall. But Biles and Raisman finished 1–2, so Douglas was left to watch from the sideline.

At 22, Raisman was older than most other contenders. A strict program focusing on diet, rest, and exercise helped her stay sharp. This paid off in the event finals. Powerful and consistent tumbling helped Raisman finish second to Biles in the all-around and floor. In most years, that would have been the standout performance of the Olympics. But as Biles demonstrated, the next wave of gymnasts from around the world continue to raise the bar.

MILESTONES

1952
The modern women's gymnastics events of balance beam, uneven bars, floor exercise, and vault are performed for the first time at the Olympics.

1976
Nadia Comăneci scores the first perfect 10 in Olympic gymnastics history, then does it six more times.

1996
The US team known as the Magnificent Seven wins team gold at the Olympics for the first time.

2008
Americans Nastia Liukin and Shawn Johnson finish first and second in the all-around at the Olympics.

2012
Gabby Douglas becomes the first Black gymnast to win all-around Olympic gold. She's part of the Fierce Five US team along with captain Aly Raisman.

2016
Simone Biles becomes the fourth American in a row to win the Olympic all-around competition. The winning US team gives itself the name Final Five.

GLOSSARY

apparatus
A piece of equipment, such as a balance beam or vault.

debut
First appearance.

dismount
A skill that ends a routine by moving from the apparatus to the mat.

horse
The firm platform gymnasts push off of during vault.

political
Being related to government leaders and laws.

technique
Skills used in physical movements.

tumbling
A set of gymnastic moves, such as handsprings or somersaults, usually done on the floor or a mat.

TO LEARN MORE

To learn more about legendary women's gymnasts, go to **pressboxbooks.com/AllAccess**. These links are routinely monitored and updated to provide the most current information available.

INDEX

Amânar, Simona, 18

Biles, Simone, 5–6, 18, 27, 29

Čáslavská, Věra, 8
Cheng Fei, 25
Chusovitina, Oksana, 26
Comăneci, Nadia, 10–11, 13

Douglas, Gabby, 25–26, 29

Johnson, Shawn, 21–22, 25

Khorkina, Svetlana, 18
Korbut, Olga, 8–10, 13

Latynina, Larisa, 8
Liukin, Nastia, 21–22, 25

Maroney, McKayla, 18
Miller, Shannon, 14–16

Patterson, Carly, 27

Raisman, Aly, 27–29
Retton, Mary Lou, 13–14

Strug, Kerri, 16–17